The Tribal Image

80 Hawaiian Islands

The Tribal Image

wooden figure sculpture of the world

William Fagg

Published for
The Trustees of the British Museum
by British Museum Publications Limited

The Department of Ethnography
(The Museum of Mankind)
is at 6 Burlington Gardens
London WIX 2EX

ISBN o 7141 1509 6
2nd edition 1977
ISBN o 7141 15460
Published by British Museum Publications Ltd.,
6 Bedford Square, London WC1B 3RA
Designed by Harry Green
Printed in Great Britain
at the University Press, Oxford
by Vivian Ridler
Printer to the University

Introduction

This is a subjective selection from the wooden figures in the Department of Ethnography, being based upon sculptural interest and quality, neither of which is a matter of scientific objectivity. It is in fact an attempt at a choice of the best pieces in this genre in the Department's very large collections, and, if such a choice cannot be made on strictly ethnographical criteria, it should at least be of considerable interest, once made, to ethnographers, since the best artists must also be the best communicators of the spiritual values of the tribe. But the artistic judgement of a museum official, who is not an artist, is unlikely to be unerring, and I called in aid to improve mine, my late friend Leon Underwood, the eminent sculptor and writer upon tribal art. Of my first selection of eighty pieces, about a quarter failed to pass the test, and were replaced by others which did. No piece has been included which he felt to be less than worthy of an exhibition chosen by sculptural standards alone. Nevertheless, I accept full responsibility for the selection, and for what is written about the pieces herein.

A word may be said about the title. The word 'image' is used primarily in the concrete sense of a representation of the human form. And all these images are products of tribal society (or more strictly of individual artists within tribal society), although there are wide variations in different parts of the world in the custom and practice of anthropologists in using and defining the word 'tribe'. In Polynesia, for example, it is rarely if ever used, no doubt because what might, in a continental land mass, be termed tribes are there isolated by geography into island groups, and are known by the names of these groups. (The dialects of the Polynesian language are also, of course, mutually intelligible, more or less, right across the vasty deep of the Pacific, though the total land area traversed is exceedingly small; but the Polynesians are not in this respect very different from the Bantu-speaking tribes which populate the greater part of Negro Africa.) The word 'tribe' is more often used in Melanesia, although a little overshadowed by island and river-system names. In Africa, too, one may find noticeable differences of anthropological practice between peoples so close as the Yoruba of western Nigeria and the Grassland tribes of Cameroon. However, such differences of usage, and even of fact, between different areas of the tribal world need not cause us any concern, for a tribe in the untrammelled state — that is before the co-ordinates of its way of life have been frozen by the arrival of a colonising Power — is in any case volatile and dynamic, constantly changing with more or less speed in the direction of fission or fusion. To expect a tribe to conform to our rigidly three-dimensional co-ordinates and submit to close definition is to misunderstand the usefulness of the term, properly used, to anthropologists and others.

The reality of the tribe is in fact best demonstrated by the examination of tribal styles in art and generally in material culture.

1 **Arawak**

Jamaica
Half-figure with 'canopy'
15¼in (39cm)
Q 77 AM1

In 1803 there was published in *Archaeologia* the following note relating to this and the next two pieces: 'April 11th 1799. Isaac Alves Rebello, Esq., F.A.S., exhibited to the Society three figures supposed to be Indian Deities in wood found in June 1792, in a natural cave near the summit of a mountain called Spots, in Carphenters Mountain in the Parish of Vere in the Island of Jamaica by a surveyor in measuring the land. They were discovered placed with their faces (one of which is a bird) towards the east.'

It is remarkable, since rather few figures in wood have been found in the Americas, that this one tribe, the Arawak, has produced so many works of supreme sculptural merit, fit to be compared with the best tribal works of the other continents, and, so far as surviving works allow us to judge, probably the finest works of wood sculpture produced in the Americas before or since Columbus.

The Arawak spread to the Antilles about the time of the birth of Christ, probably coming from the north coast of Venezuela, and lived there in the peaceful pursuit of agriculture until the Carib arrived shortly before Columbus and conquered the Arawak, incidentally becoming the eponymous originators of the word 'cannibal'.

2 Arawak
Jamaica
Bird man
34¾in (88cm)
Q 77 Am2

This is the bird-faced figure mentioned
in the note of 1803. Nothing more is
known about the significance of the
piece. These three pieces are all in
exceptionally hard and heavy wood,
much heavier for example than
mahogany. Nevertheless, they are sur-
prisingly well preserved considering
that they were found exactly three
centuries after the Discovery. Probably
they had been made at some time not
very long before 1492. During the time
of European contact the Arawak had
hereditary chiefs, a series of social
classes, priests, and gods known as
zemi.

3 Arawak
Jamaica
Standing figure
40½in (103cm)
Q 77   Am3

The awe-inspiring character of this
deity derives partly at least from his
ithyphallism. Of the four Arawak
sculptures presented here at least three,
it will be noted, present this trait; it
may be that a sculptor, choosing a
posture for his effigy of a god, might
find it natural to portray him in an act
of creation. Alternatively, it may have
been intended simply as a power
symbol. In this figure there seems a
certain echo between the forms of the
nose and the genitalia.

4 Arawak
Dominican Republic
Seat in the form of a male figure
28½in (72cm)
9753

It is impossible to describe this figure
as reclining, so dynamic is its posture.
It has been suggested that, although
the Arawak originated from northern
Venezuela, they learnt the art of wood
sculpture from Yucatan in Mexico;
yet those who think so must be hard
put to it to find examples of equally
vigorous figures in the wood sculpture
surviving there.

This piece, presented to the British
Museum in 1876, had been found in
a cave at Isabella, thirty miles from
Puerto Plata, Santo Domingo; the cave
was believed to have been inhabited
by Indians in former times. The piece
was at one time the property of General
S. Imbert of the Dominican Army.

5, 6 Witoto
Probably north-eastern Peru
Figures of a man and woman
48¾in (124cm) and 45in (114cm)
1914   4–16   140, 141

These two figures, of which almost
nothing is known, appear to come from
the area between the Upper Amazon
and the Putumayo River, on the borders
of Peru and Colombia. Their felicitous
resemblance to mediaeval English
brasses, perhaps of a helmeted knight
with his coiffed lady, may perhaps guide
us (without postulating any connection)
to the probable function of the
sculptures.

7, 8 Nootka
Vancouver Island, British Columbia
Two figures of women with children
15in (38cm) and 6¼in (16cm)
NWC 66, 62

These admirable carvings are something of a mystery to Americanists since there are no similar pieces to compare them with. Although they are not clearly documented, there is a strong presumption that they may have been collected either by Captain Cook or by Sir Joseph Banks. A publication nearly a century ago identified them firmly, although on unknown authority, as from Nootka Sound.

9, 10 Nootka
Vancouver Island, British Columbia
Two figures of women with children
6½in (17cm) and 10½in (27cm)
NWC 63, 64

The figure holding a child in a cradle
appears to have a somewhat more
owlish face than the style of the other
three pieces would justify in a woman;
this may therefore represent a spirit,
or perhaps is intended as humour.

The bold manner in which the strokes
of the knife or adze are left unsmoothed
suggests the technique of the Grassland
tribes of Cameroon.

11 Haida

North-west Coast of America
Figure of an injured man
22in (56cm)
1944   Am2   131

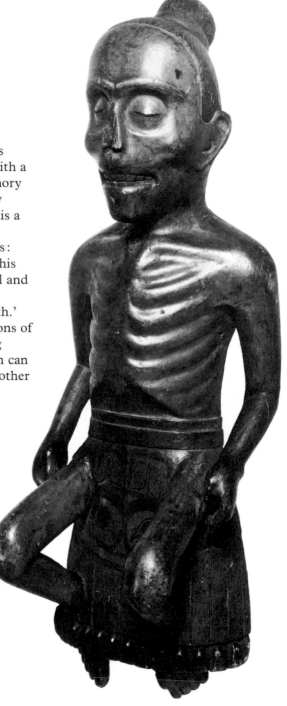

This fine Haida work is from the
Beasley Collection, to which it was
added in 1932; it was presented with a
large part of the collection in memory
of Mr H. G. Beasley by his widow
in 1944. At the back of this figure is a
label of the Missionary Leaves
Association, which reads as follows:
'HYDAH MEDICINE MAN: This
man was lost in the woods: He fell and
broke both legs, and was found as
represented here — starved to death.'
   America has yielded few traditions of
figure carving in wood, but among
them are a number of works which can
hold their own very well with the other
continents.

12 Bijugo

Bissagos Islands, Guinea-Bissau,
West Africa
Seated figure of a man
17¼in (44cm)
1970   Af18   1

In Africa, too, there are vast areas,
including almost all of southern and
eastern Africa, in which figure sculpture
is unknown. But beginning with the
Bijugo near the extreme western point
of Africa there are innumerable
traditions of figure carving in wood
throughout West Africa and almost
continuously throughout the Congo and
Angola as well.

This noble figure, very recently
acquired but undoubtedly of considerable age, may be reasonably
described as an ancestor, provided that
it is understood that the crude term
'ancestor figure' covers a multitude of
nuances of connotation.

Bijugo art is among the most
favourable in all Africa to the develop-
ment of sculptural originality, being
comparable to that of the Fang of
Gaboon.

13 Bijugo
Bissagos Islands
Standing figure of a man
18½in (47cm)
1970 Af18 2

The same style as the last here gives opportunity for an original treatment of the standing figure, which may be contrasted, for example, with the next piece.

14 Mende
Sierra Leone
Standing figure of a woman
46½in (118cm)
1901 7–22 1

This figure seems to take the grace of which the Mende style is capable to the ultimate degree, and many good judges have considered it the most beautiful of all Mende figures. It was collected before 1901 by T. J. Alldridge, an early pioneer of the ethnography of Sierra Leone. Such figures are said to be used in the curing of sickness by a women's secret society. Such societies have much greater power among the Mende than elsewhere in Africa and their women are almost alone in using carvings in their rites; they do indeed use them far more than Mende men, but they do of course go to male carvers to commission the works.

15 Dogon

Bandiagara Cliffs, Mali
Figure of a woman
19½in (50cm)
1956 Af27 1

This piece, collected in 1935 by
Labouret, belongs to the oldest type
of Dogon carvings — those which are
indefatigably attributed to the Tellem
by dealers and romantics, although
there is little more warrant for the very
existence of the Tellem, outside fairy
tales, than for the Trojan origin of the
British kingship.

It was presumably made as a dance
staff since it has no means of standing
erect. The arms are raised above the
head in what is sometimes interpreted
as a prayer for rain. The crusty
surface is the result of sacrificial
applications of millet gruel.

This piece is one of the finest in the
magnificent collection given by Mrs
Webster Plass in 1956 in memory of her
late husband, which has done so much
to diversify and strengthen the African
collections of the British Museum.

16 Mossi
Upper Volta
Standing figure of a woman
27¼in (69cm)
1969   Af3   2

Carved figures are extremely rare among
the Mossi, although found fairly
frequently as superstructures to masks.
This fine figure has a somewhat ghostly
or dream-like presence and probably
belongs to the broad classification of
ancestor figures.

17 Dan-Gio
Central Liberia
Standing figure of a woman
23¼in (59cm)
1970   AfI   8

The Dan tribes of Liberia, Ivory Coast
and Guinea are a large complex of
tribes in which the tendencies revealed
in their art suggest that a process of
coalescence was under way in the
nineteenth century which, but for the
intervention of European powers, might
well have led to a closer association.
Among these tribes masks are by far the
most popular subjects of art and fall
into two main types, a restrained and
naturalistic one associated with the Dan
group of tribes, and a violent and
grotesque type associated with the
Ngere tribe, although there are many
cases where both of these types are
found co-existing in a single village
and even where the same man has
carved both types of mask. In the
figures, however, a much greater
homogeneity is evident: they all appear
to be in the style of the Dan type of
mask.

It is particularly difficult, unless they
are documented, to suggest the use of
figures. Some are indeed effigies of
dead parents, some are surrogate
figures for chiefs who are sick or away
on tour, and some again are said to be
portraits of pretty girls.

18, 19 Baule
Ivory Coast
Pair of standing figures, a woman and
a man
11in (28cm) and 12½in (32cm)
1969   Af9   2, 1

These two figures are said to have been
discovered on the Ghana side of the
border, but would certainly have been
made in the Baule country a little way to
the west. One figure has as a neck
ornament, a British colonial sixpence
dated 1901. Most Baule figures are
deeply influenced by European contacts
but these two, which are unusually
small, are quite free from the somewhat
meretricious qualities of some of the
others and indeed show a fine feeling
for sculpture.

20 Yoruba
Western Nigeria
Dance staff in the form of a woman
23in (58cm)
1956   Af27   207

The Yoruba are not only the largest but
the most prolific in art of all the West
African peoples. They have innumerable cults each with its prescribed
works of art, and one of the most
powerful and widespread cults is that
of the thunder god Shango. His
principal symbol is the double-axe
motif, seen here on a beautiful dance
staff used in his ceremonies. The
originality of the sculpture may be
gauged from the fact that no other
piece like it is known among the many
thousands of Yoruba pieces in Europe
and America; for the same reason it is
difficult to suggest a place of origin
for it among the different carving styles
or substyles of the Yoruba.

This piece, collected about 1908 by
the first Chief Justice of Nigeria,
Sir Raymond Menendez, is another
work from the Plass benefaction of 1956.

21 Urhobo
Mid-West Nigeria
Fetish figure, a quadruped with human
superstructure
39in (99cm)
1949   Af46   188

The Urhobo are the southernmost of
the Edo-speaking peoples to which the
Bini of Benin belong. This is one of
their characteristic works of art, a fetish
figure called *ivbri* and representing a
protective spirit, probably belonging
to a family, to which petitions may be
made for various purposes such as the
finding of lost goods, success in war,
etc. The quadruped is described as an
elephant, although having no trunk;
the large figure is the head of the
family and the smaller figures are
junior members. The theory is that
they are shown in the act of honouring
or sacrificing to the impersonal
spirit figure.

22 Ijo
Niger Delta, Nigeria
Standing figure of a man
38¼in (97cm)
1952   Af26   1

This figure was collected by John Main,
an engineer stationed in the Delta,
between 1891 and 1901, and was
presented in 1952 by his son. There is
no documentation which would show
what the figure represents. The top hat
suggests a chief, but could simply be
a way of doing honour to a familiar or
protective spirit.

The styles of art of the western and
eastern Ijo prescribed so precisely what
figures and masks should look like as to
leave little room for individual variations, but there is always room for the
subtler forms of artistry.

23 Ibo
Eastern Nigeria
Standing figure of a man
6¾in (17cm)
1950 Af45 380

24 Ibibio
Eastern Nigeria
Standing figure of a man
10½in (27cm)
1914 6-16 15

This remarkably monumental miniature wood carving was given to the Museum by P. Amaury Talbot with the great collection which he made between 1907 and 1916 but unfortunately failed fully to document. It is probably from the Owerri area and is of a kind used in the magical curing of certain diseases.

This beautiful little figure was collected by P. A. Talbot in the Eket district before 1914, since when such old-style Ibibio carvings have become exceedingly rare. The somewhat benign appearance may well belie the purpose for which such pieces were used by the *Ekpo* and *Idiong* Societies.

25 Oron

Calabar, South-East Nigeria
Standing figure of a man
17in (43cm)
1956   Af27   231

This piece (again from the Plass gift,
and again collected by Sir Raymond
Menendez about 1908) is one of the
rare examples known outside Nigeria of
the ancestor carvings of the so-called
Oron clan of the Ibibio; they seem,
however, to have sufficient differences
in culture to be classified as a tribe on
their own. A vast collection of nearly
600 of these had been placed, on loan
from the owner families, in a new
museum at Oron, but could not be
accounted for after Federal troops
reoccupied the area of the former
Biafra; they had apparently been
evacuated from Oron itself at an early
stage in the civil war. Later, about a
third of them were recovered, but the
remainder seem to have been lost.

These figures are of various dates
from about 200 to 50 years ago, when
they ceased to practise their highly
individual style and had their ancestor
figures made for them by the Ibibio
carvers. They were formerly placed on
shrines out in the open. This is an
unusually small version and may date
from about the 1890s.

26 Igala
Northern Nigeria
Horned carving with figures
70in (178cm)
1949 Af46 192

This is the largest known specimen
outside Nigeria of works for the *ikenga*
cult, or cult of the hand (in the sense of
a man's power to cope with practical
difficulties), which is widespread among
tribes of the centre of Nigeria from the
Igala through Benin and Ibo country
and down as far as the Ijo of the Niger
Delta. This example is perhaps for a
very 'big' man (seen in the right-hand
view, with his principal wife at left) or
perhaps it could be the *ikenga* of a large
family. The style of carving is characteristic of the southern Igala villages
from Idah south to the Ibo border, and
in fact, although these big carvings
are especially characteristic of the Igala,
the style seems to have been adopted
from the neighbouring Ibo of the area
north of Onitsha. There are many
sacred and other symbols carved among
the figures; the basic requirement of an
ikenga (or, in Igala, *okega*) is a pair of
horns, which dominate the upper part
of the carving.

27 Idoma
Northern Nigeria
Figure of a seated woman with a child
24¾in (63cm)
1962   Af1   1

This figure was purchased from the estate of the late Sir Jacob Epstein, both for its own sake as a fine example of Idoma culture and for a particularly interesting association in Epstein's own work. The head of the infant is placed in an unnatural position, sideways on the neck. From this insignificant germ would seem to have sprung the dramatic conception of the head of *Lazarus* in New College Chapel.

The figure probably represents a primeval ancestor of the tribe.

28 Tiv
Northern Nigeria
Standing figure of a man
45in (114cm)
1969   Af9   3

This piece is almost certainly the finest
piece of Tiv sculpture known. It is from
the collection of the late Eric Bedford
and was collected in the first years of
this century. It is of exceptionally hard
wood, probably a form of red camwood,
and is one of the very few exceptions
to the rule that all ebony or similar
carvings are made for tourists. It may
either be an ancestor figure or a tutelary
spirit to protect a village.

29, 30 Mumuye
Northern Nigeria
Standing figures of a man and a woman
18½in (47cm) and 18¾in (48cm)
1922 6-10   2, 3

An administrator, Captain E. S. Lilley, presented these in 1922 with elaborate documentation on the uses to which they were put and attributing them to the Chamba. They are ancestor figures, not of primeval but of immediate ancestors, and are taken to the grove where the ancestors' bones are placed after exhumation a year or so after death; after remaining beside the skull for a day they are brought home and kept in the house; thereafter, whenever food is prepared at home a little is set aside for the image. The extraordinary process which the male figure has instead of an abdomen appears to be a three-legged stool, perhaps here referring to the status of a chief.

More recent research has raised the question of whether this style is that of a Mumuye subtribe rather than the Chamba. It is indeed quite possible that the Chamba obtained such figures, or some of them, from their neighbours; and it is true that most other Chamba figures approximate to pole sculpture with the arms carved in low relief on the surface. If so, then the remarkable conception of the enclosure of one form within another (especially in the female figure) would belong to the Mumuye. Lately, many sculptures in this tradition but mostly twice as big and a good deal less impressive have been coming out of Nigeria by illegal means and, need-

less to say, without documentation — so much so that they were at first nearly all attributed to the Chamba on the strength of Captain Lilley's documentation of these two pieces! Professor Arnold Rubin has produced to us the first adequate confirmation for the Mumuye attribution.

31 Jukun
Northern Nigeria
Standing figure of a man
34½in (88cm)
1909 2-19 1

The original documentation attributing
this piece to 'Munshi' (the Tiv) appears
evidently incorrect and it was
reattributed thirty years ago from its
resemblance to another piece assigned
to 'the Ashani', in an exhibition at
Lagos; these, however, have not yet
been traced, though they were said to
be near the Cameroon border. Professor Arnold Rubin, who has an
excellent knowledge of the Upper
Benue Valley, suggests plausibly that
the piece is in a Jukun style of the
nineteenth century. This is a very old
piece, as was the only other known
piece of the type, and the style may well
now be long extinct. A number of pieces
recently found among the northern
Jukun, however, would seem to be
closely related. This magnificent piece
was given by Dr Parsons in 1909.

32 Bamileke
East Cameroon
Standing figure of a man
37in (94cm)
1954   Af12   2

The Bamileke are one of the three main divisions of the Grassland tribes of Cameroon and their art is even more extrovert than that of the other tribes. This appears to be a male ancestor figure from one of the south-eastern Bamileke tribes. The art of the Grass-lands is remarkable for vigorous movement.

This was presented by Mrs Webster Plass and was formerly in the collection of the late sculptor Leon Underwood.

33 Bamum
East Cameroon
Standing figure of a man
22¾in (58cm)
1970   Af20   1

This very unusual figure was obtained recently in Fumban, the capital town of the Bamum, but probably originated from one of the provincial areas of the tribe. Its beamish expression should not be relied upon to suggest that it has a comic purpose.

34 Fang
Gaboon
Standing figure of a man
23¾in (60cm)
1956   Af27   246

The Fang are by common consent
among the greatest of African carvers.
This is an outstanding example of their
best work. The heads and figures carved
in this style are used as guardians of the
bone-boxes of the immediate ancestors
on the family shrine, and there is evidence that the figures themselves
represent primeval ancestors of the tribe
or the clan rather than the immediate
ancestors whose names and genealogies
are remembered. (It stands to reason,
in African as in Western thought, that
a hypothetical unnamed ancestor who
lived, say, three-quarters of the way
back to the beginning would not be
selected for such celebration.) This is
one of the finest pieces in the Plass
collection presented in 1956.

35 Bateke
Congo-Brazzaville
Squatting figure of a man
18in (46cm)
Q 74   Af663

This piece was collected by Dr
R. Hottot in September 1906 from the
Basisse clan in Luoko village, Bula
N'tangu, while he was in the Congo
as a doctor, and deposited by his widow
in 1950. Some of these figures are
ancestor figures but others are true
fetishes, that is they are not made in
honour of any particular spirit but are
powerful in themselves and made for
a particular purpose, good or bad.

36 Bena Lulua
Zaïre
Standing figure of a woman
16½in (42cm)
1956   Af27   267

This is one of the finest known works of the Bena Lulua. It is one of those collected by Frobenius in 1906 and was formerly in the Hamburg Museum für Völkerkunde. It was presented by Mrs Webster Plass in 1956.

Bena Lulua figures of this size and upwards are all said to be older than about 1888, when it seems that their use was discontinued. Up to that time the tribe was known as Baluba-Kasai, since they acquired the name of Bena Lulua only when they migrated about that time to the environs of Luluabourg. These figures are known as *lupfingu* and are in the nature of protective figures.

37 Bajokwe
Zaïre
Standing figure of a man
13½in (34cm)
1969   Af9   5

This very fine carving (lately in the Eric
Bedford collection) is of the type recently
identified by Mme Bastin as representing a Lunda chief whose name was
Chibinda Ilunga in the early days of
Lunda and Bajokwe history. The Lunda
had built up a considerable empire
some 300 years ago or more under their
king Mwata Yamvo, and they employed
the Bajokwe on more or less menial
tasks such as carving figures for their
use. In fact, it is said that all the
carvings formerly attributed to Lunda
are really Bajokwe works. This is one
of the finest extant versions of the
subject.

38 Bakuba
Zaïre
Standing figure of a woman
11½in (29cm)
1908   Ty164

This, like the next piece, is part of the
magnificent collections formed
between 1907 and 1910 among the
central Congo peoples by Emil Torday
at the request of the British Museum.
It is described as a house charm of the
Bangendi subtribe.

39 Bakuba
Zaïre
Squatting figure of a man
24¼in (54cm)
1909   12-10   1

This is the most famous of all Bakuba
statues, being the representation of the
king who is most celebrated in their
traditions, Shamba Bolongongo, ninety-
third king in the traditional list, who
reigned early in the sixteenth century
(and according to recent research may
very well have come into the Bakuba
country from outside and usurped the
throne). Most important innovations in
Bakuba culture, which is indeed higher
than that of the surrounding tribes, are
attributed to Shamba, and he is said

to have made a journey to the west to fit himself for the kingship. Precisely at this time it appears that the Bakuba were in contact with the Kingdom of Kongo, whence they learned to make fine embroideries in a closely related style. One of his most celebrated innovations was the introduction of the game of skill called *lela* (Arabic *mankala*) as a way of eradicating games of chance; this is commemorated in the *lela* board which is carved in front of him. Shamba is indeed the great culture hero of the Bakuba.

It is not quite certain that this statue is contemporary with Shamba, since it is possible that if the original portrait had decayed, perhaps about 1800, it would have been thought necessary exceptionally to make a copy of it. Only one such portrait was made during the lifetime of each king, and after his death it played an important part in effecting the transfer of his wisdom to his successor, who slept with it by his head for several nights. The piece was given to Torday for the British Museum by King Kwete Peshanga Kena in 1909.

40 Baluba

Zaïre
Standing figure of a woman
18in (46cm)
1910   441

This is one of the most beautiful works
of the Baluba Hemba, a central tribe
of the former Baluba confederacy, who
were also the most famous sculptors.
It is an ancestor figure as are most of
the figure carvings of the Hemba. Such
figures were always plied with palm oil
by women of the household until a
really deep patina was present; and
indeed the piece now gives off oil
continuously. It was collected before
1910 by a member of the London
Missionary Society. (The Bahemba are
now classified by certain Belgian
scholars as a tribe distinct from the
Baluba, but this does not seem
plausible on the artistic plane since
their style is the most characteristically
Luba of all.)

41 Baluba
Zaïre
Stool supported by a kneeling figure of
a woman
20½in (52cm)
1905   6–13   1

There are about twenty pieces known in
this highly distinctive style, but only
a little more than half of these are by
the great master whose work this is.
The remainder lack the depth of feeling
of the original master, and in place of
it have a somewhat pawky Disneyesque
humour. Moreover, the best ones are
all in a very light wood as here, whereas
those of the copyist, who may have
been a pupil of the master, are all in
hard wood. All the pieces seem to have
been collected in the first ten years of
this century. In two of these cases they
are said to have been collected in the
village of Buli which is about fifty miles
west of Albertville, half-way up the
western shores of Lake Tanganyika.

42 Baluba
Zaïre
Standing figure of a man
27in (69cm)
1949   Af46   192

This fine figure, representing an
ancestor, is a characteristic example of
the tendency of the art of the Baluba,
and especially of the Baluba Hemba, to
gravitate towards forms based on the
sphere. Here, for example, is a com-
position based on three such spheres,
presenting a strong rhythm; and indeed
it may be observed among the Hemba
that the best sculptures are those in
which the clearest approximation to
spherical forms occur. It may be
mentioned in passing that the same
applies to the masks of the central
Baluba, the most important of which,
the type known as *kifwebe*, is probably
the only example of an African mask
which is a hemisphere.

43 Baluba
Zaïre
*Headrest supported by a pair of
women (?) wrestling (?)*
7½in (19cm)
1949   Af46   481

44 Baluba
Zaïre
*Headrest supported by two female
figures*
6½in (16cm)
1956   Af27   270

Here again is a work of a master carver, this time of the Shankadi subtribe, a famous though anonymous artist from whose hand about fifteen or more pieces are known. Like the Master of Buli he was flourishing during the early years of this century. His works are always interesting for their ingenious solutions of self-imposed mathematical problems. He is known as the 'Master of the Cascade Coiffures' (which are peculiar to the Shankadi subtribe). In the Museum collections there is a second piece by him.

This delightful work by a great artist of the Hemba subtribe forms part of Mrs Webster Plass's gift of 1956. The figures seem to represent two young sisters with arms interlocked. This piece has been much used and shows a good deal of wear on the foreheads of the girls, presumably through being laid on its side when not in use. These headrests serve the function of pillows when the owner has his or her hair made up into an elaborate coiffure which it is necessary to keep off the ground when sleeping.

45 Basongye
Zaïre
*Standing figure of a man looking
sideways*
21¾in (55cm)
1908   6–22   164

This piece was collected by Torday in
1908 in Batempa's village, where he
obtained a good part of his Basongye
collections. All Basongye figures appear
to be fetishes, that is impersonal
machines (in the form of human figures)
for the control of the life force; it does
not appear that they ever use ancestor
figures. They are employed for various
purposes like those of the Bakongo,
many hundreds of miles to the west
at the mouth of the Congo. This one
has a fetish horn (of a goat) containing
medicine; rarely, as here, the heads of
the figures are turned to the left or
right, but the meaning of this we do
not know.

46 Bambole
North-eastern Zaïre
Hanging figure of a man
47½in (121cm)
1954   Af23   Q

Rare indeed are figures which are not
only made to hang rather than to stand,
but are sculpturally conceived so that
they could not be anything else. This
piece has the special added quality of
appearing to be rising in the air, like
Epstein's great lead sculpture of the
Madonna and Child (to which we shall
also have occasion to compare a superb
work from the Pacific in No. 70).
Bambole figures, from the region to the
south of Kisangani or Stanleyville, are
unique in African art (though possibly
paralleled in part by the Haida figure
of the medicine man who starved to
death, No. 11) in being representations
of hanged transgressors against the rules
of secrecy of their secret society, the
Lilwa. It is said that the wooden figures
are substitutes for the actual smoked
and dressed bodies of such malefactors
which were formerly hung on the
walls of the *Lilwa* meeting house.

Works in the Bambole style are quite
rare, and are almost all masterly. This
piece is perhaps the most impressive
of all.

This figure forms part of a magnificent gift consisting of some
thousands of specimens from all over
the world which were presented to the
British Museum in 1954 by the
Trustees of the Wellcome Historical
Medical Museum.

47, 48 Azande
Eastern Sudan
*Standing figures of a man and
a woman*
31½in (80cm) and 20½in (52cm)
1949 Af46 522, 523

These are the largest pieces known in
this remarkable style which was
flourishing at the end of the last
century in an area where there was little
carving, namely the district around
Yambio on the southern border of the
Republic of Sudan. The style has some
evident affinities with that of the
Mangbetu in the neighbouring part of
the Congo. The unique conception of
arms and shoulders as a near-circle is
one of the marks of this style.

49 Zulu
South Africa
Figure of a man
24¼in (62cm)
1954 Af23 Q

Zulu carving is not usually very
adventurous, being largely confined to
very simple figures of ancestors and
carvings on walking sticks, etc., but
this piece (and one or two others like
it) show that they could on occasion
surpass most other tribes in abstract
sculpture.

50 Kalash
Chitral, West Pakistan, on the
Afghanistan border
Equestrian figure
22in (56cm)
1944 As6 1

Our last African example and our first
Asian are curiously related by the
circumstance that the tribal peoples of
both areas were formerly known as
Kafirs — from the Arabic word for
'infidel'. Most of Kafiristan was con-
verted to Islam in 1895–6 and was
then renamed Nuristan, the land of light.
The Chitral tribes, however, remained
pagan. They made lifesize figures for
the graves of their dead, and kept
smaller replicas of these in the villages.
Erection of the large figures is accom-
panied by a festival which is very
expensive. Neckrings of brass, iron,
etc., are worn by both sexes and are
represented on most of these effigies.
A pointed head-dress represents a
male turban (according to Dr H. Siiger)
and presumably the two-pointed head-
dress in this case is also a man's turban.
Women are shown wearing a horned
head-dress. Pieces of this kind are still
being made by the Kalash tribe in
Chitral, whence they were often brought
by members of the British Army in
India.

51 Melanau

Sarawak, Malaysia
*Squatting figure holding a smaller
figure*
22¼in (57cm)
1905   786

This figure represents a spirit named
Belam who catches the souls of sick
people and returns them to their bodies.
Severe illness is caused by the soul
leaving the body and treatment consists
of rites designed to persuade it to
return. Some illnesses are thought to be
caused by possession by evil spirits
and in this case rites are performed to
entice into the house a spirit powerful
enough to cast out the spirit which has
entered the sick person. Belam is one
such spirit. While in a formal sense it
might be described as a mother-and-
child figure, it may in fact be shown in
the act of returning a soul to its body.
Moreover, the figure itself may be male,
to judge by the cap.

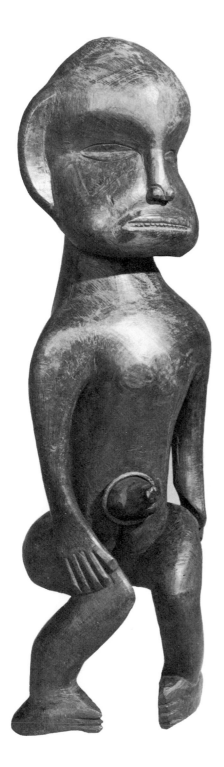

52 Lelak

Sarawak, Malaysia
Standing figure of a man
24½in (62cm)
1905   641

The Lelak are one of the numerous
tribes scattered through Sarawak and
Borneo generally, which present considerable diversity of language and
culture, though some authorities have
thought that these tribes, formerly
called Klemantan, have the best claim
to be regarded as the aborigines of the
island. There is no documentation for
this figure, which like the last and
the succeeding one, comes from the
great collections formed by Dr Charles
Hose in Sarawak at the turn of the
century.

53 Kenyah
Sarawak, Malaysia
Twisted figure of a man
17½in (44cm)
1900   1043

The Kenyah tribe are found on both
sides of the border between Sarawak
and Indonesian Borneo to the south.
This figure represents Bolli Atap,
a spirit who protects a house against
sickness and attack, and is called upon
in cases of madness to expel the evil
spirit possessing the afflicted person. It
may indeed have been an architectural
ornament, to be attached, for example,
to the end of a beam.

54 Nias

Off the west coast of Sumatra
Seated figure of a man
27½in (70cm)
59   12-28   168

The people of Nias live in autonomous
villages which were formerly at war
with each other, human heads being
taken for revenge or for use in sacrifice.
On the death of any important man or
woman who leaves male descendants,
a wooden figure is carved. The village
priest after placing rice and some of
the deceased's clothing on the grave
catches any spider which appears on the
grave as it is thought to contain the
soul of the dead man. The spider is
taken home and released near the image
which the soul is then thought to enter.
If a crack should appear in a figure,
the soul is thought to have left it and
the process is repeated again. The
ornaments on the figure symbolise the
rank and achievements of the deceased.
A beard, for example, means that he
was an old man of some authority,
while a necklace shows that he was
noted for bravery.

   This is from Sir Stamford Raffles's
collection made in the East Indies
about 1815.

55 Leti
East of Timor
Seated figure of a woman
22½in (57cm)
1954   As7   184

The people of Leti live in small villages,
herd cattle, and cultivate rice. Each
family has an image of its ancestor,
usually placed on the roof beams of the
house. The protection of the ancestor
is invoked by the father of the family
and offerings are placed in bowls in
front of the image. An image of the
founder of the village is placed in the
village centre and the chief, who is
descended from that ancestor, invokes
his protection on behalf of the whole
village. Ancestor worship plays a major
part in the religious life in this part of
Indonesia.

   This piece is from the great
benefaction of the Trustees of the
Wellcome Historical Medical Museum.

56 Igorot
Philippines
Standing figure of a man
30in (76cm)
1914   4–14   65

Only one in twenty of the population of
the Philippines is not civilised in a
western sense. The Igorot of Luzon are
among the best known of the remaining
tribal groups. The Igorot living in the
Kiagan area are also called Ifugao by the
Bontoc Igorot, who live in large towns.

Their ancestor figures are called
anito. They are kept in the houses, and
the skulls of slain enemies are offered
to them; feasts are instituted in their
honour on the spot. When people are
disappointed in them, the images are
beaten or pierced with spears or
thrown out of the house.

The figure finely brings out the
ghostly or dreamlike quality appropriate
to spirits of the dead.

57 Igorot
Philippines
Figure of a man
16¾in (43cm)
1954   As7   204

This again is from the great gift of the
Wellcome Historical Medical Museum.
It appears like the last to be from the
Kiagan area.

58 Undetermined Tribe
Philippines
Standing figure of a man
21in (53cm)
1954   As7   203

It has not been possible to identify this sculpture as from a specific island of the Philippines. The arms in this case are, exceptionally, carved separately, though the shape of the junction with the shoulder is so designed that they cannot be placed in any other position.

59 Igorot
Philippines
Squatting figure of a man
33½in (85cm)
1954   As7   274

This design, of a man squatting with
elbows to knees, is a motif very
frequently found in the whole South-
East Asian area, especially through most
of the islands and into New Guinea.
Within this area it is likely to have been
due to diffusion, but there is no reason
to suppose any connection with the
numerous other places in the world
where this unpatented body posture
occurs.

60 Iatmul
Northern New Guinea
House post in the form of the figure of
a man
103in (262cm)
1964 Oc6 1

This is the centre post (or rather the top
portion of it) from a cult house of the
western Iatmul, near Ambunti in the
middle reaches of the Sepik River. It is
a piece which, by New Guinea
standards, is of considerable age. It was
brought back from fieldwork in the area
by Mr Anthony Forge.

61 Sepik River Tribes
Northern New Guinea
Squatting figure of a woman
9¾in (25cm)
1936 7–20 171

In 1936 the British Museum received
the most generous gift of a large number
of works of art collected in the New
Guinea area during the recent voyage
of the late Lord Moyne, who had
carried out a great deal of valuable
research work in many areas which had
previously been unrepresented in the
Museum's collections. This small figure
is at once one of the most delightful
and one of the most powerful of the
sculptures which he brought back with
him on his yacht *Rosaura*. Its precise
purpose is not known.

62 Bosman
Ramu River, Northern New Guinea
Standing figure of a man
11½in (29cm)
1936 7-20 83

This is another of the proceeds of Lord Moyne's expedition and is a particularly good example of the Ramu and Sepik Rivers style, especially in the treatment of the bird attributes which are highly characteristic of the area. The Bosman tribe are in the delta of the Ramu River about twenty miles eastward from the delta of the Sepik itself.

63 Torres Straits Islands
South coast of New Guinea
Figures of a woman and a man in copula
10in (25cm)
+2,500

Sir Augustus Wollaston Franks was the Keeper of Antiquities in the British Museum for most of the second half of the nineteenth century, and was one of the greatest of all the benefactors of the Departments into which the Department of Antiquities has subsequently divided. In the case of Ethnography, there was a long period, especially in the seventies and eighties, when his name appeared as donor of a very high proportion of the acquisitions of this Department from all sections of the world. He had a fine unprejudiced eye for sculpture from areas such as this in which the opinion of his day would not have admitted that sculpture could exist. The figure was described as a 'god of procreation' (the masculine presumably subsuming the feminine) and it is said to have been used for love magic. One is reminded, though with a reversal of roles, of Tibetan bronzes representing a god with his *sakti*.

64 Fly River Tribes

Southern New Guinea
Standing figure of a man
51in (127cm)
1906   10-13   41

This piece, which is from the important
collection given by Major W. Cooke-
Daniels in 1906, appears to come from
the Papuans at the mouth of the Fly
and is said to be an agricultural charm
used in the gardens. It is probably made
from the root of a mangrove to judge
by its characteristic curved form. No
explanation is evident for the turning of
the head to the right, unless it is to
show the vigilance of the image in
watching over the safety of the crops.

65 New Ireland
Melanesia
Standing figure of a man
41½in (105cm)
1944 Oc2 1801

The *malanggan*, or figures carved in
New Ireland for ceremonies performed
to honour the ancestors and to display
the wealth and increase the prestige of
their descendants, are widely admired,
but considered as sculpture the great
majority of them are already in a
decadent phase in which the emphasis
has shifted from form to an excessively
fussy decoration. There would seem to
be no place in good sculpture for
camouflage; its result is that the
sculpture atrophies. This carving, on
the other hand, appears to belong
(whatever its actual age) to a stage
before that of most of the known
specimens (themselves eclipsing in turn
the works of fifty years later): the forms,
interior and exterior, are bold and the
body is clearly seen through the curtain
of fish and animal attributes.

This is another piece from the great
gift of the late Mrs Beasley; the
Cranmore Museum, which her late
husband maintained during his lifetime, was particularly strong in
Melanesian art.

66 New Ireland
Melanesia
Standing figure of a man
45¾in (116cm)
1936   11–23   1

Although this figure was collected on
Wuvulu or Maty Island (nearer to New
Guinea), it is clearly in the New Ireland
ula style (not that of the *malanggan*); it
was presented in 1936 by A. Lockwood,
Esq. The breasts, which might suggest
hermaphroditism, are probably
exaggerations of male breasts, as very
often in Africa.

67 New Hebrides
Melanesia
Figure of a man, upper part
19¼in (49cm)
1944   Oc2   1056

This unique piece, sawn from a large
figure or a pillar, suggests to us, by the
benevolent intensity of its presence, that
it was an ancestor figure with protective
functions towards the living. But
Melanesian ancestors are notoriously
fickle and should not be thought of as
predominantly benevolent. The piece
may come from the Banks Islands.

68 Trevanion Island

Santa Cruz Islands, Melanesia
Seated figure of a man
8in (20cm)
1944 Oc2 1170

The island of Trevanion or, to give it its
vernacular name, Te Motu, is the home
of a fine though little-known tradition
of sculpture associated with a shark
cult. This piece, from Nelu village, is
said to represent the shark spirit Men-
ar-ta-lu. The spikes at his wrists are
said to be used for pulling the sharks
out of the water and hanging them on
shore. A fine collection of these rare
figures forms part of the late Mrs
Beasley's gift.

69 Luangiua Island
Ontong Java Atoll, Solomon Islands,
Melanesia
Standing figure of a man
16¼in (41cm)
1944 Oc2 1729

Ontong Java, though administered as
part of the Solomon Islands, is one of
the Polynesian 'outliers' — Polynesian
colonies which, in their diaspora, settled
on islands within the Melanesian area.
This figure, which appears to be made
to hang rather than stand, is further
advanced in abstraction than would be
found amongst Melanesian groups.

70 San Cristobal Island

Solomon Islands, Melanesia
Standing figure in the form of a man
28½in (72cm)
1904   6-21   14

This sculpture is indeed made in light
wood, but it has the rare sculptural
gift of appearing to take all weight off
the feet and to be in the process of
ascending (like Epstein's *Madonna and
Child* in Cavendish Square). It was
collected between 1890 and 1893, and
is said to be a door ornament representing a sea spirit. The figure appears to
have for feet a pair of gambolling
dolphins, or perhaps sharks, and other
fish for hands. The human face also
forms the snout of a monstrous diving
shark, whose tail rises above.

71 Maori
North Island, New Zealand
Standing figure of a man
36½in (93cm)
1950 Oc11 1

This wonderful old sculpture is far
removed from the world of metal tools
and the surface decoration is beautifully
varied and unmechanical. The figure
is in fact a burial chest or repository
for human bones known as *papa koiwi*.
It was collected in the mid nineteenth
century on the Auckland Peninsula,
probably from the Bay of Islands,
where the majority of other known
specimens of the type were found in
caves near the coast.

72 Maori
New Zealand
Standing figure in the form of a man
67in (170cm)

This appears to be wholly without
documentation and bears no registra-
tion number, which may indicate that
it entered the Museum before about
1850. It is carved from a red dye wood,
and the carving seems to be free of
metallic influence. The decorative
work is not, as in so much Maori
carving, in conflict with the form, like
ivy on an oak.

73 Tahiti
Society Islands, Central Polynesia
Standing figure in the form of a man
21in (53cm)
7047

The Sheffield Literary and Philosophical
Society presented this piece in 1871.
It was collected between 1821 and 1824,
and probably represents a sorcerer's
familiar spirit. The major gods were
represented in Tahiti by rather abstract
forms, often barely recognisable as
human — the well-known 'sinnet
gods'; the more realistic figures such as
this one appear to be for lesser spirits
invoked by sorcerers.

74 Easter Island
Eastern Polynesia
Standing figure in the form of a man
18½in (47cm)
4835

After the great stone figures, the best-known antiquities of Easter Island are these *moai kavakava* or 'emaciated men'. Their true significance is long forgotten, perhaps before 1850, but it appears to be established, from the surviving aetiological myths, that they are some form of ancestor figures. It is not quite certain whether they represent old men before or after death. They are not made to stand but to hang from the person of the owner, who sometimes had ten to twenty of them; they were worn in dances at feasts, and the more a man wore, the more likely were his requests to the god to be granted. This piece was acquired from a dealer in 1868.

75 Rarotonga
Cook Islands, Central Polynesia
Standing figure in the form of a man
27¼in (69cm)
LMS 169

This is part of the great collection made
early in the nineteenth century by the
pioneer missionaries of the London
Missionary Society to illustrate the
errors of the heathen, although not
without some admiration of their
artistry, and later made over to the
British Museum. Although an attached
label identified the piece as the god
Te Rongo and his three sons, it more
probably represents another god such
as Tangaroa, the sea god and creator.
Only one other such figure is known.

Homage to the British Museum

There is a Supreme God in the ethnological section;
A hollow toad shape, faced with a blank shield.
He needs his belly to include the Pantheon,
Which is inserted through a hole behind.
At the navel, at the points formally stressed, at the
      organs of sense,
Lice glue themselves, dolls, local deities,
His smooth wood creeps with all the creeds of the world.

Attending there let us absorb the cultures of nations
And dissolve into our judgement all their codes.
Then, being clogged with a natural hesitation
(People are continually asking one the way out),
Let us stand here and admit that we have no road.
Being everything, let us admit that is to be something,
Or give ourselves the benefit of the doubt;
Let us offer our pinch of dust all to this God,
And grant his reign over the entire building.

(Reprinted by permission of the author,
William Empson, and Chatto and Windus.)

76 Rurutu Islands
Austral Islands, Central Polynesia
Standing figure in the form of a man
46in (117cm)
LMS 19

This, the prize of the LMS collection,
was quite differently identified by the
two missionaries mainly concerned in its
collection: William Ellis, who seems to
have been the actual collector on
Rurutu, published it in 1829 as a
representation of Taaroa (Tangaroa),
the creator and sea god of the Polynesians, in the act of creating gods and
men; John Williams, who received it
on Raiatea, said in 1837 that it was A'a,
national god of Rurutu. Both mention
that the back of the figure is detachable
and the body hollow. When it was given
up it was filled with twenty-four or
more small images, which may have
been put there to absorb divine power.
Later, when it was deposited in the
British Museum in 1890, it was known
as Tangaroa-Upao-Vahu — Tangaroa-
up-in-the-sky — a designation presumably received from the LMS.
This attribution seems a little the better
established, and perhaps a little more
appropriate to the finest extant work of
Polynesian art.

   The sculptor has used a form of the
Henry Moore 'eye' (seen in his works
of the 1950s and after) which is also
found, though rarely, in Pre-Columbian
America and Africa.

   This piece has been celebrated in
William Empson's poem (opposite).

77 **Hawaiian Islands**
Northern Polynesia
Standing figure in the form of a man
82in (208cm) — with base 105in (267cm)
39   4-26   8

This and two similar figures — at the
Bernice Pauahi Bishop Museum at
Honolulu and at the Peabody Museum
of Salem, Massachusetts — may well
be the largest surviving wooden figures
from Polynesia. They all represent
Kukailimoku, the war god of the family
of King Kamehameha, an avatar or
specific form of Ku, the war god of the
Hawaiians (Tu elsewhere in Polynesia).
Here for once we may be fairly sure
that we are right in seeing a fierce
expression in the face, which here
appears to extend down to the feet. It
was given in 1839 by W. Howard, Esq.

78 Hawaiian Islands
Northern Polynesia
*Standing figure in the form of a
human*
16¼in (41cm)
1944 Oc2 716

The Hawaiians were pre-eminent
among the Polynesians for the dynamic
character of their sculptures, as this and
the two following pieces amply
demonstrate. Vigorous movement is
suggested potentially rather than by
arrested motion. This fine piece, from
the Beasley collection, came 'from the
royal *marae*, or stone-paved temple, at
Karakakua'.

Hawaii was populated from the
Society or Tahitian Islands before
AD1000 and thereafter had little contact with anywhere else until the advent
of Europeans. Nevertheless, their
language changed remarkably little,
though their art, and the rest of their
material culture, developed a real
originality which seems never to have
ossified into conformism.

79 Hawaiian Islands
Northern Polynesia
Bowl supported by three acrobatic figures
8in (20cm)
54   12-27   119

80 Hawaiian Islands
Northern Polynesia
Figure in the form of a woman (?) dancing
26½in (67cm)
1657

The strength which underlies the apparent chubbiness of much Hawaiian art is one of its most remarkable features, and is well seen here. The piece is identified as a salt dish (*pa inamona*). It has been in the British Museum since 1854.

Either this piece or one remarkably similar was seen in 1779 by some members of James Cook's third expedition who visited an important temple, said to have been the Hale-o-Keawe at Honaunau, Kona. Their description speaks of a figure 'resting on his toes and fingers, and his head inclined backward; the limbs were well proportioned, and the whole was beautifully polished'. The Superintendent of the City of Refuge National Historical Park at Honaunau suggests that the piece may have reached London on the *HMS Blonde*, whose officers removed images from the Hale-o-Keawe in 1825. It appears to have entered the great collection of Henry Christy before (possibly a little after) that collection's transfer to the British Museum on his death in 1865.

Yet it has been noticed (first, possibly, by Mr John Read when making a film in the British Museum on Henry Moore's work some years ago) that the figure displays its extraordinary merits to far greater effect when standing (which it does with perfect balance) than when in the prone position: the front of the body has far more dynamic sculptural interest than the back, but this is seen only in the standing posture. To suppose that the prone position is the only correct one is to suppose that sculptural excellence — particularly when of the universal kind — can be accidental. The all-fours position has been said to be one of the postures of the *hula* dance; the standing position is a startling evocation of a dancer passing into a trance or semi-trance state, the neck temporarily dislocated, as anyone will recognise who has seen this

phenomenon in other parts of the world. Could it not be that Cook's men saw it in its normal resting position, but that, as the climax of some ceremony, it would be raised with dramatic effect to the upright stance? It is true that there is no evidence for this, but we are extraordinarily lucky to have an eye-witness description of it even in one position (at rest), and there is no account of it during the ceremony. Finally, the soles of the feet are flat; but if the figure were not meant to stand, this flatness would be avoided by any sculptor anywhere in the world, and above all by the sculpturally conscious Hawaiians.

In the sculptural exploration of space through spiral motion — not generally attempted by tribal artists — the Hawaiian masters join with the other great innovators on the North-west Coast of America and in the Grasslands of Cameroon.

See also Frontispiece.